DIVINE
DIRECTION

22 Inspirational Devotionals for Hope, Healing, Breakthrough and Transformation

D1280685

A Collaboration Organized by

BENECIA PONDER

DIVINE DIRECTION
22 Inspirational Devotionals for Hope, Healing, Breakthrough and Transformation

Published by ILLUMINATION PRESS
Atlanta, GA

Unless otherwise noted, Scripture quotations are taken from The Holy Bible, New International Version®, NIV®. Copyright © 1973, 1978, 1984, 2011 by Biblica, Inc.® Used by permission of Zondervan. All rights reserved worldwide. www.Zondervan.com. The "NIV" and "New International Version" are trademarks registered in the United States Patent and Trademark Office by Biblica, Inc.® Scripture quotations marked CEV are taken from the Contemporary English Version. Copyright © 1991, 1992, 1995 by American Bible Society. Used by permission.

Scripture quotations marked (AMP) are taken from the Amplified Bible, Copyright © 2015 by The Lockman Foundation. Used by permission.

Scripture quotations marked (MSG) are taken from The Message. Copyright © 1993, 2002, 2018 by Eugene H. Peterson. Used by permission of NavPress. All rights reserved. Represented by Tyndale House Publishers, a Division of Tyndale House Ministries.

ISBN: 978-1-950681-99-0 (paperback)
ISBN: 978-1-950681-98-3 (ebook)

Collaboration Organized by Benecia Ponder
Edited by Karin Crompton
Cover and Interior Design by August Pride, LLC

QUANTITY PURCHASES: Schools, churches, professional groups, clubs, and other organizations may qualify for special terms when ordering quantities of this title. For information, email to inspire@inspirationalauthors.com.

ILLUMINATION PRESS
Benecia Ponder
1100 Peachtree Street | Suite 250 | Atlanta, GA 30309

HEY THERE!

Welcome to Divine Direction— the first book in the Inspirational Devotionals series! I'm super excited you're here!

Your picking up this book is not an accident. Even now, you are experiencing Divine Direction.

I encourage you to approach this book in whatever way feels right to you. The stories can be read in order from beginning to end or at random. Either way, take time to pause and reflect on the story and its message before moving on to the next chapter.

I pray that something in these stories impacts and inspires as you journey to your own hope, healing, breakthrough, and transformation!

Love & Blessings,

Benecia

· · · · · · · ·

I pray that the eyes of your heart may be enlightened in order that you may know the hope to which he has called you, the riches of his glorious inheritance in his holy people, and his incomparably great power for us who believe.

Ephesians 1:18-19

· · · · · · · ·

TABLE OF CONTENTS

LEARNING TO LOVE PEOPLE

Kelly McCausey

There was a time I claimed I wasn't a "people person." I also often said, "I'm just not a joiner." I believed these statements were true, but it turns out – they weren't at all.

I was born in 1966, in the midst of the Vietnam War. An accidental pregnancy from the affair of a young wife and mother waiting for her husband to come home from war. Told in no uncertain terms to get rid of me, she arranged for my adoption, and I became the youngest child of Ted and Beverley.

I was raised to know about my adoption and had positive thoughts and feelings about it as a very young child. I was special, wanted, chosen! Those feelings metamorphosed into something very different as I experienced years of physical and emotional abuse from my mother.

We didn't go to church and had no faith to speak of at home. But I knew about God and the devil from television and books. I prayed God would take me away from my mother and give me back to the "real" mom who must love me. When that didn't work, I called out to the devil, offering him my soul if he'd kill my mother and set me free. I was eight at the time and that didn't work, either.

I knew my father was an alcoholic; he drank beer and got goofy. I didn't discover until after I left home that my mom was an alcoholic, too. She hid it behind "iced tea" and bottles in her closet. Finding out she wasn't just mean – she was drunk and mean – helped. (A little.)

As I hit my teens, I cultivated that sense of being unwanted. As a young adult, I made choices that drove it all deeper. At twenty-eight, when I met a Christian woman who treated me like family and expressed joy in the midst of rotten circumstances, I confronted the idea that there might be a God who wanted me.

I considered myself an atheist and too smart to fall for

faith, but I was curious about my friend's happiness and bought myself two cheap Bibles (having been startled to discover there was more than one at the store.) Over the next few weeks, I read, I talked with my friend, and I wondered if I could believe.

I could, and I did. I asked Jesus into my heart.

Next, my friend said, I needed a church. She was moving out of state and recommended a church in town she'd heard good things about. When I walked into that little community church as a single mom with a young son, I was terrified. I wasn't a people person. I wasn't a joiner. My faith was so new.

Fast forward. I joined the church. I got really involved and ultimately took a job on staff working in the office. I still had an internal identity that said I was not wanted. Oh, I knew God wanted me – that truth came with faith. But people? Ugh…people! Even at church, people are people and sometimes they really hurt others.

I held my walls up and avoided situations that made me vulnerable. Friends at church begged me to attend a retreat known for melting hearts and helping people find deeper connection. I was a big no and when an older gal came to again ask why I didn't want to go, I said, "People suck!"

She wrapped her arms around me. I thought it'd be that

garden variety church hug and gave her a little squeeze in return. When I expected her to end the embrace, she tightened her arms and did not let go. I went from uncomfortable to panicky. I swear she turned her hug into a vice grip – and she whispered, "All people don't suck, Kelly. Some people are amazing…like you."

Something deep inside me broke in that hug. She held me as tears poured out and I melted into those arms of love and acceptance.

It would have been so easy for that woman to feel my rejection as a personal one and to have left me to my isolation. Thank God she didn't. She brought God's word to life with her arms that day.

. . . .

Romans 15:7 says:

"Accept one another then, just as Christ accepted you, in order to bring praise to God."

. . . .

I went to that retreat, and it changed my life. I left a people person. I left a true joiner. I left more whole than I'd ever been.

We are always growing and changing and becoming more of what God created us to be -- unless we simply refuse to. Don't refuse.

. . . .

Father God,
Help me to find the willingness to see where I've been
refusing change. Open my heart to the people, hugs,
and other opportunities to heal and grow into all You've
designed me to be. In Jesus' name, Amen.

. . . .

Kelly McCausey knows you want to pub-
lish content you're proud of for a community you love and that takes a strong
mindset. Her Love People + Make Money
blog and podcast offers you resources
that help you build that mindset and
make wise choices about your content
marketing.

I WILL
give them an
UNDIVIDED
HEART
and put a
NEW SPIRIT
in them;

I WILL
remove from them
THEIR HEART
OF STONE
and give them a
heart of flesh.

Ezekiel 11:19

AWE AND WONDER
Paula Ames

I woke up to raindrops on my window yet again. It was day four of a torrential downpour in Los Angeles, which is not the norm -- perhaps I should have anticipated something unusual.

I waited for a brief break of sunshine and hurried out the door with McDougal and Linus, my two rescue pups, in tow. They hadn't been getting their usual walks due to the constant rain, so we had to make it happen when we had the chance.

As we walked down the driveway, I noticed a single leaf in the gutter of the sidewalk. The fragrance of wet asphalt and fresh adventure was in the air. The dogs were pulling, anxious to get down the hill to smell all the smells. In reverence, I was stopped in my tracks.

One of my favorite pastimes is finding hearts in nature, whether it's a rock or a tree stump or something else with a stamp of love all over it. However, this leaf was a whole new level of God's remarkable hand. I knew it was filled with an important message, but I wasn't sure what to make of it.

The rain had made the neighborhood appear greener than ever before. As I looked at the trees in my neighbor's yard and across the street, there wasn't a dead leaf in sight. And yet, I was staring at this faded, brown, dead leaf with a bright green spot in the middle in the shape of a heart. I was left perplexed.

We continued our walk as I marveled at this leaf that God had so obviously laid in my path.

But why?

I'd been in a season of frustration, confusion, and loss, spending my days job hunting and trying to reinvent myself, but not quite sure of my next step. Paralysis and uncertainty had become constant companions, as I'd been laid off three times in the past seven years of my sales career. I was ready for something new. I had just been reading Isaiah 43 and was focused on Jesus doing a new thing in the wilderness when God sent me that love note.

I was fasting from everything sweet and leaning into God's whispers, though questioning if I could really hear from God when I so desperately wanted to. Everything seemed upside down and then, the bottom completely fell out. The same week I was given that miraculous leaf, I lost my younger brother, Teddy. It was sudden and unexpected, and the news threatened to crush my soul like nothing I had ever experienced. My emotions were raw and wrapped up in guilt, sorrow, and regrets. I longed for more -- more time, more energy, more love, more opportunities. I was having a hard time making sense of it all.

It was the darkest year of my life and yet, through the grief or perhaps because of it, a great courage rose up along with a sense of urgency that can only come from deep loss. I found myself saying yes to some big God ideas that, like a Jonah Girl, I had long been running away from, and I accomplished things I had procrastinated on for years.

There are some lessons and revelations from God that can often only be realized in hindsight. I now understand that God is always speaking to us in various ways when we have the audacity to listen.

In the face of many regrets, I hold tight to knowing that on one particular morning, I stood tall and I said yes. One of the last texts I sent Teddy was just a few days before he died. I had a nudge from the Holy Spirit to reach out to him. I want to tell everyone what I told him: I hope you know that God will never love you more because of what you do, and He will never love you less for what you do – He truly loves you right now, no matter what.

That is who our God is. That is the Jesus that I serve. God is love. We can't earn our way into Heaven. God freely gives us access to Him because of His love and ridiculous grace. 1 Corinthians 13 says, "Love never gives up, never loses faith, is always hopeful and endures through every circumstance." The Message version affirms that Love never dies.

As I stood up in front of hundreds of people who had come to honor my brother, I was overwhelmed by the love in the room. I shared the invitation of the leaf: Live your life in awe and wonder and rest assured that there is immeasurably MORE ahead from a God who wants us to know that there is life after death and the best is yet to come.

. . . .

Father,

Thank You for welcoming me into more of You. Fill me up with Your desires and speak to my heart the truths that You know I need to hear. I am so grateful that my loved ones are right where they need to be, in Your Presence Lord. Hold them tight and lead me to walk in Your ways and to follow Your heart for me. In Jesus' name, I pray. Amen.

. . . .

Paula J. Ames is a ferocious lover of life who follows after the heart of Jesus. A sales and marketing professional by day and a creative entrepreneur by night, she loves putting pen to paper, decorating her Craftsman bungalow home, and creating mixed media art. A true California girl, she enjoys spending time near the ocean sticking her toes in the sand and conversing with God. She resides in Los Angeles and is a proud Dog Mama of three silly rescue pups.

See,
I am doing
a new thing!
Now it springs up;
do you not perceive it?

I AM
MAKING A WAY
in the

WILDERNESS
AND STREAMS
IN THE WASTELAND.

Isaiah 43:19

3
ꓳOY ꓔROM THE INSIDE OUT
Cheryl Graham

I stopped dead in my tracks one day at work. I stood in the middle of the nursing unit, unable to think clearly. I couldn't grasp what was happening to me. My hair had recently started falling out. I was always sluggish and tired. I had hand tremors. I was consumed with anxiety and often felt my heartbeat in my throat; I'd wake up with my bed soaking wet with sweat.

But the worst thing? My face was plastered with cystic acne – hard, red, painful pustules that made me shrink down and lose my confidence. Forty-two and going through acne AGAIN? That was horrific.

My goal has always been to help others, and I was pursuing that goal with everything I had. I enjoyed making a difference in people's lives. I just didn't realize the harm I was causing to myself. One year, I worked 360 days of twelve-hour shifts; I was helping others but forgot about myself.

I was also in a marriage going nowhere. I had recurring nightmares about being in a car with my husband, trapped in a tornado sinking deeper and deeper into the funnel. I had to get out and make changes. I needed to find peace in this part of my life, so I decided to end things. I finally put myself first and let the peace I needed come to fruition.

Perhaps that strategy could help me with my health concerns too, I thought.

After the divorce was final, I went for a much-needed physical. I was diagnosed with hyperthyroidism, a condition in which the thyroid gland produces too much of the hormone that regulates your metabolism. My vitamin D level was low, which accounted for a lot of other symptoms I was having, including the brain fog. I immediately started taking medication for the hyperthyroidism and some high-dose Vitamin D to get me back to being "Cheryl."

Every two or three weeks, I'd be back in the endo-crinologist's office having lab work done and getting my medication adjusted. At the same time, I looked for what else I could do to make myself feel and look better. I started using clean botanical products to help clear up that horrific acne and made some changes in my diet, including using some nutritional products. I began to have more energy and felt better; I could think more clearly.

The biggest change was in my skin – there was less redness, fewer inflamed pustules and fewer breakouts, and I could touch my skin without it feeling like it was on fire. Something was happening and I was excited!

My lab work kept getting better, and my thyroid uptake scan came back normal; my doctor couldn't believe what he was seeing and didn't understand what was going on, but I did. I had made a change for myself after being reluctant for so long.

During one visit, the doctor sat me down as he reviewed my labs. I was face-to-face with him and the room was silent. He blurted out, "You must have a brain tumor. There's no other reason for your labs to be trending towards normal."

I quickly and adamantly rejected this and explained, once again, the changes I'd made in my life. He didn't believe it and scheduled me for an MRI, which was negative.

I knew what happened: God dropped a gift in my lap. I knew in my gut I had to trust Him. I was here for whatever God wanted to do in me.

I started to take a more active role in my spiritual life and more blessings started coming my way. I was living a Proverbs 3:5-6 life and I wasn't looking back. I kept doing what I was doing, and my life completely changed.

My journey brought me to Atlanta, Georgia, and this new season has been so rewarding. I feel so much better -- more energized and more in tune with my mind, body, and soul. I am amazed at my transformation, but I didn't do this alone; God was there with me. With Him by my side, I had the courage to step out on faith and follow what He placed in front of me.

I've been on this transformation journey for nine years. I started waking up earlier to begin my day with prayer, meditation, self-affirmations, and essential nutrients, feeding my mind, body, and soul. By mastering my mornings, I put myself first. I realized I couldn't pour from an empty cup; there'd be nothing left to give.

Today I am healthier and more vibrant, and on my way to living a life fulfilled.

Lean into your faith. Be open and listen to God, and let Him move you in the direction you need to head. He will never steer you wrong. Trust that God has our best interests at heart; He wants what is best for us ALWAYS. He's our biggest supporter and will guide us. Follow His lead and we'll go places we hadn't even imagined.

. . . .

Heavenly Father,

I praise You because You know all things. I thank You that I can trust myself, my loved ones, my health, my finances, my dreams, and my needs into Your hands.
I trust You Father. Keep me trusting.
In Jesus' name I pray, Amen.

. . . .

In April of 2012, a health scare was the catalyst that drove Cheryl to begin her wellness journey. In addition to herself, she set out to help her peers develop goals to reach their optimal wellness. In June of 2012, Cheryl started her own Health & Wellness business. Her passion is to show her community that by developing a stronger mind, healthier body, and through achieving inner balance, we can increase our health span and become our best selves!

I will be

GLAD
AND
REJOICE

in you;

I WILL

SING

the praises of your name,

O Most High.

Psalms 9:2

4

SOMETIMES JOY FINDS YOU

Kathy Haynie

In August 2016, I celebrated my sixth wedding anniversary to Mike, a man who was an answer to my prayers. Just two short weeks later, my husband passed away from a massive heart attack. I was left to take care of our family alone.

I hardly slept, which stressed my body and caused my fibromyalgia to consume me with pain. My body went into "robot-mode," and I could only do what absolutely needed to get done. I couldn't focus on myself; there was no time for that. My family needed me.

Five weeks after losing my husband, my dad passed away. I felt like an orphan: no mother, no father, no husband, and no best friend. A spirit of heaviness came over me, and I knew it was depression because I had been in that dark place before. This time I couldn't even try to fight it. I was numb and had no clue how to express anything. The kids needed to be taken care of, so I just focused on what needed to be done for them.

The day-to-day struggles and lack of sleep took a toll on me. I began missing church on Sunday mornings because I hadn't fallen asleep until daybreak. Then more shock: my fifteen-year-old daughter told me she was pregnant. I wasn't happy, but I couldn't change it. I needed to take care of things because my daughter needed me, and so did my grandchild. I wouldn't let my daughter go through this alone.

When I confided this news to the ladies in my Sunday school class, I thought I was sharing with people who cared about me. Instead, my family was shunned by our church family. A lady I admired and considered a mother figure asked me why I had been missing Sunday mornings. After I explained that I wasn't sleeping much and had a hard time getting up, and that my fibromyalgia was causing me pain, she said she didn't believe that was the reason. My pastor told me people understood I was having trouble with my kids. I felt like no one cared or wanted my family there.

The holiday season from Thanksgiving to New Year's was awful. I didn't feel like celebrating any of it but did so for my family. I continued in robot-mode for months, lacking emotion and unable to believe that change would happen anytime soon.

It took a few years for me to emerge from that dark place because I felt alone and empty inside. I had no church, no friends, and I had no clue where God wanted me to be. I knew that my granddaughter wasn't a mistake, and I couldn't picture my life without her. I also knew that I needed and wanted to be back in church, but I was left searching for a place to belong.

During my search, God brought me to a women's Bible study group where I met some amazing Spirit-filled women. They were my support and my friends. As my spiritual connections were strengthened, I realized that I needed to forgive those who hurt me before I could fully heal. They were wrong to treat me that way, but I was wrong to let them keep me from serving the Lord the way I once did.

Once I forgave them, the heaviness that consumed me slowly began to lift. The more I stepped out of my comfort zone, the clearer I saw things.

Sometimes when you least expect it, joy finds you. I had to open up and share my story -- the pain, the confusion, and the loneliness -- in order to heal.

Is there anyone in your life that has caused you pain and hurt, that you are having a hard time forgiving? If so, I urge you to pray and release it to God. Tell God that you forgive them and pick up the pieces of your life, one piece at a time.

Lord,

You are my hope when times are rough. When I face heavy burdens, thank You for lifting me up and giving me a hope for the future. Please bless me and help me to grow in my knowledge of You.
In Jesus' name, I pray. Amen.

Kathy Haynie is a mother, grandmother, and widow. But more importantly, she is a child of God. Kathy tries her best to always honor her Lord and Savior. Kathy lives in North Alabama and enjoys traveling and seeing the beauty that our Heavenly Father creates. When times are hard, and there seems to be no answers, Kathy looks around to find some sort of beauty from the chaos that life brings. Sometimes all Kathy can find is the shape of the clouds in the sky, but that reminds her that God is there. He is always there.

He put a

NEW SONG

in my mouth
a hymn of praise to

our

God.

MANY WILL SEE AND FEAR
THE LORD AND PUT
THEIR TRUST IN HIM.

Psalms 40:3

5

CHOOSING HOW TO SHOW UP

Lady Rayven Monique

Iremember the specific moment that my family noticed I had changed.

My son and daughter were in the car with me, both young teenagers at the time, when we pulled into the parking lot of a grocery store. The parking spots had no barrier between them, so I pulled through the original spot I drove into, intending to park in the facing spot so that I wouldn't have to back up to get out.

As I pulled through into the second spot, a woman

honked her horn. When I glanced up at her, she was visibly upset, making obscene hand gestures and shouting angrily. I couldn't hear the words she was saying, but I could see that she was saying them, and my guess was they would make a sailor blush.

She was further down the aisle, and it looked as though she had come around the corner to take that exact spot. Though I had gotten lucky and found a pull-through spot, the parking lot was quite crowded, and it was apparent that she was very attached to the spot I now occupied.

I hadn't seen her before I pulled through, but as soon as I did see her, and all the rage she was hurling, I put my car in reverse and backed up, giving the spot to her.

My children watched the whole exchange, captivated. As soon as I had re-parked, my daughter, stunned, asked, "Did you just reward bad behavior?"

That was one of my favorite sayings as my children grew up: "We don't reward bad behavior." They knew better than to throw a fit and expect to get their way – I simply didn't respond well to it. I once postponed Christmas for an entire day because my children were cranky and unappreciative.

And yet, here I was, giving up what was arguably my parking spot to a grown woman throwing a temper tantrum in her car.

I looked at my daughter and said, "You know, it looks like she's having a much worse day than I am."

I remember in that moment that I didn't feel angry with this woman for her gestures or honking. I didn't feel embarrassed that I hadn't seen her and had mistakenly taken a parking spot she claimed. I remember simply feeling compassion for her – to be so upset about such a little thing; there had to be something much bigger going on that I would never know about.

And I remembered being in this same parking lot going to this same grocery store not too long before that day, just minutes after saying my final goodbyes to our dog, Sadie, and how surreal it felt doing something so basic and normal as grocery shopping when I had just held her head in my arms as she passed away at the veterinarian's office across the street.

I had no idea what was going on in that woman's life, but in that moment, I prayed she would find peace. My children, on the other hand, were still in shock.

They didn't grow up with a mother who had compassion for a raging stranger. No, the mother they grew up with had created the saying, "We don't reward bad behavior" as a direct reminder to herself. I was the one who displayed bad behavior the most in my household.

When I was younger – from my teenage years until my early thirties -- I suffered from really bad PMS. I say that I suffered, but in reality, those who lived with me were doing most of the suffering. I had the reputation in my house of having a bad temper and being completely and inappropriately irrational.

And honestly, I was – for about two days a month. I hated it.

The worst part was being in the moment and literally forgetting that PMS existed. Like clockwork, for forty-eight hours, I would feel like everyone was out to get me, that my life was in shambles, and that no one understood me. There were lots of tears, hurt feelings, and usually yelling. I would be so caught up in feeling this way that I would not associate it with any hormonal symptoms. I wasn't aware, in the moment, that there may be a reason for feeling the way I did.

So, how irrational did I get?

One time in my late twenties, I was angry at my then-husband for something I don't remember today. His form of arguing was to remain silent, which didn't pair well with my form of arguing, which was to become louder and more dramatic until I was acknowledged.

I remember feeling so frustrated that I wanted to destroy something, so I took a kitchen knife and shredded the screen of the sliding glass door. He had just replaced it the day before, so this was my act of violence against him. In the moment, it made so much sense to me, but coming down from the hormones the next day, I realized with great clarity that I was out of control.

That was the day I decided I didn't want to do it anymore. So I did one very simple thing that completely changed my life: starting that day, I began to chart the day of the month most likely to be the day that PMS would strike. I put a simple gold star sticker on that day on my calendar.

That one act helped me to remember that PMS existed while I was going through it. If I started to feel irrational, I'd remember to glance at the calendar and look for that gold star. And when I found that it matched the day (which was ninety-five percent of the time), I was able to let go of the symptoms and the destructive behavior.

It was slow at first and didn't always work, but as time went by, the simple awareness of my PMS chaos caused it to disappear in me. Within a year, when it would hit, within minutes I was able to shrug it off, knowing what it was, and I was able to get on with my day incident-free.

If you met me today, you'd probably never dream that I was capable of being labeled someone who had a bad temper.

Awareness is very powerful. It restores our power and control over our lives and our futures.

It's the gift of being conscious -- in the moment -- that we all have a choice about how we want to show up, and what impact we want to have, because we're always having an impact, whether we know it or not.

· · · · · · · ·

Dear God,

Create in me a clean and willing heart. Change me from
the inside out. Help me to reflect Your
goodness in all I do. Amen.

· · · · · · · ·

Lady Rayven is a doer in life - she does
things that others can't, or won't. A
true original, she's manifested incredible adventures, ranging from touring the
country for 6-years with her family in an
RV, to meeting her soul-mate, to deliver-
ing 9 babies as a surrogate mother. Rayven believes that happiness is our natural
state of being, and guides others to man-
ifesting their own dreams. She lives in
Florida on a 5-acre permaculture home-
stead.

Do not conform
to the pattern of this world,
but be

TRANSFORMED
by the

renewing of your mind.

Then you will be able to

TEST AND APPROVE

what God's will is

HIS GOOD,
PLEASING
AND
PERFECT WILL.

Romans 12:2

6

LOVING LIKE JESUS LOVES

Crystal Reilley

If we look back on our lives, God has always been right by our side walking us through whatever issues we faced. Ever since I was a little girl, I have seen more darkness than I care to describe here, but I know that God has protected me repeatedly, and I put my faith and trust in Him.

In April of 2003, my husband and I got married in a beautiful ceremony filled with laughter, love, and joy. Imagine getting dressed up in a beautiful gown and being so excited to have all your loved ones surrounding you on your big wedding day. After the celebration, we let some close family members stay at our home while my husband and I stayed in a hotel.

I will never forget that night. A terrible call interrupted my state of bliss. Something horrible had happened at my house. The police had been called and I was told to get home right away.

When I arrived, there was chaos. My uncle and father had been drinking and in their inebriation, a violent disagreement erupted. My neighbor had called the police after hearing loud shouts and seeing a fight on my front lawn. I walked into the house and saw the path of destruction the fight had taken from my kitchen through the front door. Yet, even with the glaring evidence, neither my father nor my uncle would admit to any wrongdoing.

I was devastated. Anger and unforgiveness consumed me for a long time. I wrote letters to my father and uncle telling them how horrible they were for fighting and ruining my wedding night.

Over the course of several years God worked on me. He softened my heart and helped me forgive. He showed me that if I wanted to be healthy and in alignment with His will, I needed to be free from anger, bitterness, and resentment.

I spent many years praying for my father and my uncle. Specifically, I prayed for God to remove the anger and bitterness from each of our hearts. I also prayed for Him to soften their hearts and fill them with love. My father and I began working to restore our relationship; my uncle refused to try.

In the winter of 2015, God prompted me to reach out to my father. During our conversation, he told me my grandmother had fallen and broken her hip. She was in the hospital and needed more medical attention. I raced to Portland, knowing my grandmother would need my help because my dad and uncle were never very good caretakers. I did what God called me to do: show up and take care of my grandma regardless of the past.

I spent weeks in Portland at my grandma's side. She gave me power of attorney to take care of her affairs and get her placed in an assisted living home. At each step, I texted updates to my father and uncle, inviting them to help make decisions regarding their mother's care.

A few weeks into my visit, my uncle called and asked me to come to his home. I didn't want to, as I knew he had been drinking and I didn't want to deal with drama, but I hesitatingly agreed.

Before I went, I called my mother.

"I don't want your opinion," I said. "I just want you to

cover me in prayer and please don't tell my husband!"

It was one of the scariest moments of my adult life. I knew my uncle got mean when he was drunk. And though his wrath had never been directed toward me before, I knew how angry and hateful he felt about me since my wedding night.

My mom prayed a prayer of protection. She prayed for God to put a filter on my mouth and only allow me to speak words that He wanted me to speak. I prayed and trusted God to empower me to meet my uncle with love like Jesus loves.

When I showed up, there was a gun on the table. It was dark and scary. I'm 5'7" and my uncle is 6'3". I sat across from him, not allowing him to think I was afraid. He spewed out more ugliness than I care to share. He hated me. He thought my husband and I tried to kill him and my dad on our wedding night. He believed that I was his enemy. He believed that my husband and I hired a hit on him to kill my family. So crazy!

Through all of my uncle's ranting, God only allowed me to respond with love. For every ugly word he said, I replied, "It's ok, I love you."

That was it. Nothing else came from my mouth. God's presence was so strong and the filter on my mouth was as well.

After being berated for a half hour, I got up and simply said, "I can't do this; obviously we will not have a conclusion. I will see you some other time."

I stood up and walked away.

I got a phone call about fifteen minutes later and he berated me again. He'd had even more to drink and kept saying horrific things. Again, I had this beautiful God filter on my mouth.

After he emptied himself of all his venom, he finally had room for the love I had to give. We talked and came to an agreement that something horrific happened on my wedding night. We decided to let it go and never mention the incident again.

Because he is a chef and makes delicious food (he catered my wedding), he said the only way to put the past behind us was if I drove back over and had a steak. I love his cooking! As tired and worn out as I was, my heart needed to have more healing. I needed my family. I needed to be fully forgiving and truly put the past behind me.

I drove back to my uncle's house and stayed the night. When I arrived, I wrapped my arms around him and repeatedly told him I loved him. He broke down and said he loved me too. He made me a steak and we started a new relationship with love. We now talk almost every day and have a very healthy relationship. That doesn't mean that things don't get brought up and feelings aren't triggered. We have set boundaries and respect that we shouldn't talk about that time in history.

Letting go of the hurt and pain caused from my wedding night. Never talking about it again. Moving forward with love that only Jesus could provide. Forgiveness for things that are truly unforgivable. Putting things in the past and saying goodbye to them so we can have a future. I wanted to be in my grandma's life. I desired to have a Daddy again and an Uncle. He was my favorite Uncle growing up. I had cherished memories from my childhood with him. To do all of those things, I had to forgive and love like Jesus loves.

. . . .

Heavenly Father,

Heal my hurting heart. Lead me to live a life of love
and forgiveness. Amen

. . . .

Crystal has a heart to serve and loves
to help women become the woman that
God has called them to be without apol-
ogy through a Christian Business Net-
working Organization called The Tapestry
Network of Reno. Crystal is an outdoor
enthusiast. She loves snow skiing, sunshine, wakeboarding, four wheeling,
razor riding, watching her children partic-
ipate in all their activities, reading, learning, and spending time with family and
friends. She is filled with positivity, love,
and an energy that she loves to share
with those who meet her.

Bear with each other

and

forgive

one another

if any of you has a
grievance against someone.

FORGIVE

as the Lord forgave you.

Colossians 3:13

7

ONE WORD
Maureen Riley

The Lord will use a single word to speak to you, training you with it and enhancing or establishing His sovereignty with it. Just like a Bible verse will work its way into your soul and spirit, a single word can become a laser beam of focus and truth.

Several years ago, I memorized Jeremiah 29:11 and, especially after my divorce, began to stand on it as a promise the Lord was making to me.

I didn't know what my future would look like in His hands, but I was learning to walk with the Lord, and I started believing that promise was true for me and my two young children. As a single parent, I have been very blessed, but it has rarely been easy.

In late 2020, my two children asked for camping equipment for Christmas, and not just any camping equipment -- they had found some high-tech tents and sleeping bags online. There's nothing more heartbreaking than not being able to give my children what they truly want. We are frugal throughout the year. My children understand our situation and are well-mannered about consumer requests, but they were passionate about these tents.

It was close to Christmas when I finally ordered them. I had been saving a little bit and the cost of these items was approximately equal to what I had on hand, so I placed the order even though it meant I had only pennies left over, as usual.

About a month earlier, I had made a different investment: in my health. For the first time in my life, I was carrying an extra thirty pounds. I was uncomfortable, sad and burdened in an existential sense that didn't align with my beliefs. Jesus had set me free! Why did I feel so down?

I approached a health coach whose journey I had been quietly observing online. "Could it be true?" I wondered. "Could I achieve the impressive results her clients were experiencing? Could I really feel like myself again?

Could I regain my energy and my positive self-image and my sense of joy?"

I decided to reach out. Her encouragement and willingness to come alongside me in my journey was enough that I found the strength to begin working on being better and healthier for my children.

I had also begun seeking the Lord to find "my word" for 2021. The answer was slow in coming, but soon after ordering these tents I listened to a sermon which was based on HOPE, specifically the God of HOPE in Romans 15:13, and I just knew HOPE was for me.

As I waited for the packages, I started to wonder whether they'd arrive in time to put them under the tree. Then came an email that a shipment was en route from Israel. I hadn't realized the tents were made in Israel; they were being shipped from a town called Shaarei Tikva.

If my Bible studies have taught me anything, it's that God never misses a chance to communicate with His children. I looked up what Shaarei Tikva means in Hebrew and could hardly believe it when I read the translation: Gates of HOPE.

I celebrated this special intimacy with the Lord all year as I leaned on the God of HOPE and trusted Him in the process of learning how to shed the dysfunctional mind-sets, unhealthy habits and patterns, and extra weight I had been carrying. Recently, I also made the joy-filled decision to partner with the God of HOPE to become a health coach and support others on this journey. As such, I HOPE the ones He's trying to reach through me will discover more than weight loss, more than community, more than better energy, more than transformed finances, more than the satisfaction of goals attained in His strength. I HOPE they discover and cultivate greater intimacy with the God of HOPE.

. . . .

I praise You Lord! You are the God of Hope!
Thank You for filling me with Your joy, peace, and everlasting love. As I trust in You, let my hope overflow so that others may see it and be blessed. Amen

. . . .

Maureen Riley obtained her BA in Psychology from Georgetown University. Always a passionate "people person," she is humbled that the God of HOPE has called her to serve the Kingdom as a Health Coach on a mission to transform as many lives as possible by helping others achieve total health: mind, body, spirit and finances. She lives in San Diego with her two children and their many pets, where she enjoys hiking and continuously learning.

May the
GOD
OF HOPE
fill you with all

joy and *peace*

as you trust in him,
so that you may
OVERFLOW WITH HOPE
by the power
of the
HOLY SPIRIT.

Romans 15:13

USING MY VOICE
Stephanie Sherwood

My story starts at a family party. Many of our family parties included both sides of our family, and I loved it; there were more people to talk to, more mushy kisses and hugs to give, and both my grandpas! I was an energetic five-year-old who loved to continuously chat and talk and ask questions. On this particular day, I was a bit more energetic than normal because what little girl wouldn't love to dip into the candy dishes at a family party when they're five? I was often told I was "too much!"

We were gathered around the table in the kitchen. I had one grandpa to my right and my other grandpa to my left. My little elbows were perched on the table while my chin was resting gently in the palm of my hands. I couldn't have been happier. I had both of my grandpas' attention at the same time and it was all about me.

Here is where the story takes a turn--I was being paid to not talk, as I was again being "too much."

To my five-year-old self, it was pure joy. I had both my grandpas and the promise of fifty cents if I didn't talk for a few minutes. That fifty cents meant when I got home, I got to walk down to the corner market with all the penny candy. I wasn't old enough to walk there by myself, so that meant a walk with one or both of my parents – pure joy again! I was over the moon.

What my grandpas meant for fun and a break on the family's eardrums, the enemy took and twisted around to steal my impact. For at that moment, my value shifted; my value was attributed to not talking. When I would muster up the courage to use my voice, there were always negative consequences. I began to not really talk to many people for fear of those consequences.

Many of my childhood memories are vague, but a few things stand out. In second grade, my teacher, Mrs. Nisten, used to say, "Stephanie, how many times have

I told you my name rhymes with listen and that is what I expect you to do!" It wasn't that I wasn't listening, I was simply asking questions. The other kids in the classroom would laugh, which would reinforce the lie I was believing, that my value was not in talking.

One day in sixth grade, I was excited to work on a group project, which meant I got to talk and chat and ask questions. I was in my element until my teacher, a large man with yellowish bug eyes, called out my name, "Stephanieee!" I wasn't the only one in the classroom who was talking, but somehow, I was the problem. He walked towards my group and stood right in front of me. Staring down at me with those bug eyes, he said in his big man voice, "I think you have done enough talking for today." Once again, the lie was reinforced. My value was in not talking.

My next memory of the lie being reinforced was when I was a young executive with Macy's. Every Friday afternoon, all the department managers would meet with the store manager for our weekend strategy. It always seemed like my hand was the only one going up to ask questions or point out a potential problem. It was never out of disrespect, but it started again--my name was spoken, "Stephanieee!" and that feeling crept back in, that my value was in not talking.

Ironically, it never failed when we gathered again on

Monday mornings, something I thought might be an issue was an issue. Hmmm...

I loved working at Macy's. My numbers were great, and the buyers loved me. Many of them felt I should work on getting promoted, which made me beyond excited and nervous all at the same time.

I needed to talk and be visible to get promoted, and as I asserted myself more at our manager meetings, it didn't go well. My manager pulled me aside and said I was no longer to say anything at the meetings unless I was spoken to directly. The lie was again reinforced.

Shortly after this conversation, we had major flooding where I live in Northern California. Macy's rallied to help our neighbors and offered an amazing discount for families and businesses affected by the flooding.

We gathered that Friday afternoon to talk about the ad that was being placed in the newspaper and how we were to identify the flood victims. I could instantly see the problems and was super excited I wasn't working that weekend. Yet I did as I was told, and I kept my mouth shut.

At our Monday morning huddle, the managers who had worked the weekend reported on all the chaos and upset customers they had. Macy's system to identify affected neighborhoods had been flawed. One of the other managers looked back at me and quietly said, "You knew this was going to happen, didn't you?" I responded with a smile and kept my mouth shut.

These stories show how easy it is to get caught up in a lie of the enemy and how it steals your impact and the calling that God has on your life.

It happens without you even being aware of it, which is just the way he desires it. He desires us small, quiet, simply going through life and rolling with it.

I didn't discover the lie until I was in my late thirties, stuck trying to move my entrepreneurial self forward. I was talking with several women who had become my champions and my community. They started asking me questions and I blurted out my Grandpa story. They were shocked.

After a few more questions and answers, one of the women said, "You feel your worth is in not talking. You are absolutely fine using your voice as long as the outcome isn't tied to you. If using your voice moves you forward towards making money, impact, or success, you simply can't use it." Now I was shocked.

After sitting with this revelation for a bit, it started to ring true. I didn't know where to begin or what the outcome was supposed to be. So, I did what many of us do when we learn something about ourselves. I did nothing with it. How could I? It was who I knew myself to be. It had become a part of my identity. Changing that seemed too difficult.

This is not my identity in Christ. The heart of being a Christ-follower is to "put off the old identity" and receive your new one. It is about becoming your TRUE SELF.

Looking back, I can see how the lie has shaped me, my actions, and my outcomes. More importantly, I can see the value in letting the lie go. It wasn't easy. Our minds go back so easily to what is familiar, even when the familiar no longer serves us and our God calling. It is something that I still work on, but praise God I don't have to work as much or as hard as I used to.

What I have come to learn and embrace (I am declaring it!) over the last decade is that God designed me with the gift to talk; not to just talk about a few things, but to talk about many things. Not to only talk about the easy things but to talk about the hard things. The things that go against culture, barriers, obstacles, and even the status quo are not off limits. I am excited to see where God takes me and my voice.

. . . .

Dear God,

Help me to honor and trust the unique way You created me. You formed my personality, my voice, and my abilities to glorify You. I release any thoughts that I am not good enough and embrace the beautiful way You designed me. Amen.

. . . .

With her heart for service, Stephanie Sherwood has always been a champion for change. Her whole life has been about supporting and building up people, teams, and communities. And like many women she has wrestled with her identity...not good enough, not smart enough and the list goes on. YET... as she continues to walk-out her life journey, she has found healing and truth is in living a transparent life. She uses her God- given voice (she was paid not to speak as a child) as a weapon against the enemy. Her life charge is to right the injustices of shame, lies and fears.

**Let's just go ahead
and be what we
were made to be,**

WITHOUT ENVIOUSLY
OR PRIDEFULLY
COMPARING
OURSELVES
WITH EACH OTHER

**or trying to be
something we aren't.**

**Romans 12:6–7
(MSG)**

9

HEALING OUR CUTS
Karen Robinson

Desperate for him to stop, I grabbed the closest thing to me, a wall calendar.

How was this supposed to protect me?

At that moment, the metal frame slid out, and I lunged forward before he could. A drop of blood fell down his face. I had cut his forehead. Stunned, I froze, thinking the worst was about to happen, but he just walked away. I finally stopped the bully.

The bully was my father.

Cutting him was a turning point in my abuse. He did not hit me again after I cut him, but the emotional abuse continued in full strength.

He named me "Bitch, Whore, Cunt, Slut," often with the F word in front of each hateful, shaming label he threw at me. I don't remember how I felt. I don't remember who soothed me or how I soothed myself. My best guess is that food was my comfort. Ice cream, chocolate, and Doritos were and still are my drugs of choice.

I may have physically cut him, but he emotionally cut me over and over. How does one recover? How did I recover?

I credit my faith for the beginning and middle of my recovery. I leaned on faith I didn't know I had. I discovered faith is a mighty tool your bully can't take away from you. Faith can be a quiet assurance or a booming, powerful voice.

Over the years, I leaned into it. I kept going and setting goals for myself. Knowing what I didn't want was also helpful. I do not want to be poor or have an unfulfilling career. I do not want an abusive partner. I do not want to be unhappy or miserable. I do not want to believe that I'm unlucky, unlovable, or not deserving of an abundant life. Even though I have deep personal wounds, I will not let my cuts or pain stop me.

Moving past cuts, wounds, and emotional pain is hard and sometimes I fail miserably. The trick is getting back up, no matter how many times you suffer. As the poet and mystic Rumi once said, "The wound is the place where the Light enters you."

When you feel like you are failing miserably, just focus on the next baby step. Know that if you stumble, someone will come along to take over for you or will carry you over the finish line. You will grow stronger with each baby step. Let your higher power carry you. Let the light enter your wounds. Refuse to be shamed by your trauma. Don't claim the shame.

If you have been working on overcoming past emotional abuse, like I have been, I know the journey can feel like a lonely walk. Sharing how the abuse affected me, how it drove me to both depression and anxiety; How I work to turn it around to create a life I love living, and how I believe you can turn your life around too and this can simply start by telling your story. Telling our stories provides us a voice and what is so powerful about speaking and writing our stories, is that you may have felt voiceless during your past abuse or hardship. Our journey doesn't have to be so lonely, and I believe sharing stories is a path to connectedness. "All sorrows can be borne if you put them into a story or tell a story about them." – Author Karen Blixen

....

Thank You Lord for Your promise to always be with me. Thank You for strengthening me and upholding me with Your righteous right hand. Thank You, that moment by moment I am kept in Your love. In Jesus' name, Amen.

....

Karen Lynn Robinson, LCSW, is a service driven social worker, therapist, and coach with 23 years of clinical experience. She received both her BSW and MSW from the University of Maine, where she was originally from. Karen is a genuine, authentic, compassionate provider. Her specialties are trauma recovery, anxiety, and depression. In her free time, Karen enjoys reading, writing, and spending time with her family.

So do not fear, for

I AM
WITH YOU;

do not be dismayed, for

I AM
YOUR GOD.

**I will strengthen you
and help you;**

I will uphold you
with my righteous
right hand.

Isaiah 41:10

10

LIGHT AT THE END OF DARKNESS
Treyonda Towns

As human beings and divine creative vessels, we've accepted the reality that, as we live, so too shall we have an experience with death. The question is, what does that look like, when the life is vibrant and full of success? What does that look like when you are searching for the correct path to walk?

In 2008, my hope and trust were tested to the utmost degree. It was a sunny spring-like day when I received those words, "You need to get here, she's gone," that will forever ring in my ears. My daughter didn't leave voluntarily. She was murdered.

How could this have happened? As a young mother, I was determined and consistent at providing a home that was patient, encouraging, motivating, safe, and full of hope. I was not going to be a statistic that said I failed. I also was intentional in providing those things that I did not have and needed as a child.

My daughter would often bring home young ladies who did not feel safe returning to what was supposed to be their home. My days were full of appointments to advocate for the rights of a young person whose rights were being violated. Yet, at the hands of those she trusted and loved, my daughter took her last breath.

How ironic that her breath was cut off and I found myself having to learn how to breathe deep and release that breath full of inner emotions consisting of hurt and disappointment wrapped within feelings of betrayal. The gateway to me accepting that death had visited my home and taken away my firstborn was blocked.

This blockage prevented me from going out to do daily duties like doctor appointments, school drop-off, grocery shopping, work, etc. without someone accompanying me. What happened to her was the implosion of all things that were within me. Fear and anxiety had their grip on me due to years of pushing down the shame, embarrassment, hurt, and rejection inflicted on me because I had been a teen mom. Anxiety nudged me to be consumed with the despair I experienced and to disappear further into the abyss of darkness in my mind.

One day while I was organizing some things in a closet, I found my beloved daughter's purse that she was carrying on that dreadful day. Her perfume, lotion, keys, other random items, and her day planner. I never knew she used a planner. That day planner became a sign to me that I must continue to live for those siblings and children left behind. But most of all, so that her legacy may go on to impact lives that had no one else to hope for them.

In John 14:8, Phillip says, "Lord, show us the Father, and that will be all that we need!" In other words, you have all you need even in difficult times -- the tragic times, the disappointing times, the lonely times, the confusing times. He is giving us all that we need in this moment to make it to our next.

So even in this living again, experiencing death at that capacity, there's a power once acceptance is allowed in. The beautiful memories of the smiles, of the laughter, of the jokes, of the surprise moments; the first words, the first steps, of bringing home the friends that were seeking solace and refuge from the negative environments they were living in.

The painful aftermath and the sting of death brought about a fire and a light surrounded by a force to push and bring the legacy of love. Recognizing that I AM is a Healer of all things that we may suffer. Diving into a deeper understanding that love is the source and the vine from the one that created all things.

I often say that every end has a beginning, and every beginning has an end. The word of God talks about a beginning void of any form of tangible existence other than darkness. Yet He spoke and said, "Let there be light." So I share these words of hope in grace to encourage others that there is life and light at the end of the darkness, even in death. I have found myself living the best life in post-death experiences after the transition of my precious daughter.

Father God,

Help me to see Your light in the midst of my darkest times. I pray that Your light and love shine brightly throughout the world. Amen.

Treyonda Towns MA, CLTC is a multi-faceted business owner, Author, Broadcast Host, Certified Trauma Recovery & Visionary Coach. Treyonda holds a degree in counseling psychology/trauma and provides supportive resources to those who have suffered traumatic experiences or loss. Treyonda also focuses a portion of her work on entrepreneurs, advocates, healing practitioners, and fellow coaches who are in a position of stagnation and unhealthy patterns of trauma-induced behavior, yet are looking for healing alternatives and tools beyond or in addition to traditional counseling services.

For God, who said,

"LET *light*

SHINE

OUT OF

DARKNESS,"

made his light shine in our hearts to give us
the light of the knowledge of God's glory

displayed in the face of Christ...

2 Corinthians 4:6

11

PASS IT ON
Cindy Beckles

As the Amtrak train approached the snow-covered Union Station in Washington, D.C., my heart sank. I had just enjoyed a relaxing ride from Florida and could not believe my eyes: the unseasonably warm temperatures in D.C. had been replaced by a blizzard.

Things had changed so much in the past two weeks. When I left for Florida, I was fixated on a fun, sunny vacation. I made a grave error by not packing properly. While away, I focused on a handsome guy that I met on a cruise; I didn't even check the weather like I usually do.

As I stood on the platform, I felt the chills. My bones were cold. I had no coat, gloves, or scarf, and I had to figure out how to survive my trip home in record-breaking snow and arctic temperatures with only flip-flops on my feet.

Due to the weather, most of the public transportation had been shut down. I was toast. I lived almost an hour and a half away, and my bus was not running. I could stay with a friend who lived closer in the city, if I could get there. I wound up waiting more than four hours for a bus to my friend's place. While I stood there freezing, one by one, strangers gave me a gray scarf, gloves, and a hat. I never asked for anything. It is amazing how God uses people to help you when you are in need. I felt so blessed they shared these priceless gifts with me.

I was so excited when the warm bus finally arrived, but as we started driving, my joy turned to fear when I saw lots of trees but no houses, lights, or cars. I just saw snow piled on every side. When I got off the bus, I took one step in the darkness and immediately sank into the snow up to my waist. The bus driver pulled away and did not look back. I could not move and thought, If God does not help me, I am going to die here.

I looked up and down the street but saw no signs of life. It seemed a bit hopeless as I prayed to God. I was freezing, but I had not lost my faith.

After a few moments, I saw a truck coming and waved down the driver, who stopped. He helped me into his truck and drove me to my friend's apartment. God had truly answered my prayers, and I have never felt so relieved. Although I have a good memory, I cannot remember this gentleman's name, nor what he looked like, but I will never forget his kindness. He was my angel.

As I stepped out of the truck, I kept saying I could never thank him enough. He just smiled and said, "Pass it on."

As I look back now, I am also grateful for the Good Samaritans who instinctively gave me the gloves, a gray scarf, and hat. To some this may only be a story, but to me it was a miracle.

Although that happened almost thirty years ago, I have rarely told this story. I felt embarrassed that I placed myself in such a dangerous situation, and I only recently told my mom and sister because I know better than to take a ride from strangers or to not be prepared. I started sharing the memory because it serves as an inspiration and a cautionary tale to me as well as to others. It feels unreal, but it really happened. I still marvel that the truck came so quickly. I have the treasured gray scarf to this day.

Telling the story reminds me of the importance of passing things on through words and deeds. We all have life-changing experiences we would prefer to keep to ourselves. These may not be our finest moments, but they could be the fuel or missing links for other people's dreams. It is less painful to tell others about our past challenges when we know these stories may help them.

Our powerful experiences are not just for us. Do you have uplifting stories? Pass them on.

Finally, this memory also encourages me to pay it forward. Just like the truck driver, we must be open to helping others. There are so many people who need assistance or just a kind word. Televangelist Joyce Meyer encourages people to do daily random acts of kindness. We can never understand completely what people are going through, but we can try. As we live each day, we should strive to give back to others. We need to "Pass it on."

Dear God,

Open my eyes to see opportunities for random acts of kindness. Make me Your Good Samaritan as I seek to show Your kindness to others.
In Jesus' name I pray. Amen.

Cynthia Beckles, MBA, loves helping coaches, consultants, and service-based businesses overcome challenges to find the right marketing strategies to propel their brand so that they can secure more clients. Her integrated marketing approach empowers businesses to implement what is best for their company, and not necessarily what is hottest. Cindy is inspired by giving back to her community. She gives 100% to everything she does. Cynthia is famous for her legendary macaroni and cheese.

Therefore,

AS GOD'S CHOSEN PEOPLE,

holy and dearly loved,

clothe yourselves with

COMPASSION,

kindness,

HUMILITY,

gentleness

and

PATIENCE.

Colossians 3:12

12

WE'RE NEVER ALONE
Jennine Carter

One day when I was home from college on break, my father asked me, "How lonely are you?"

Much like I remember the first time my mother said "I don't know" in reply to a question, I remember the room of the house we were in and the sensation of the floor dropping away beneath me.

He didn't ask, "Are you lonely?" or any of the other deeply introspective questions my emotional reactive armor can detect, deflect, and defend against. He asked, "How lonely are you?" as if some level of disturbance and disconnection was a foregone conclusion.

I suppose I should not have been surprised. I have watched my father, a psychologist and pastor, patiently and relent-lessly reduce strangers to tears – even a car salesman once - by holding up mirrors to their souls. Oddly, as vis-ceral as this memory is, I do not recall whether I answered his question or suddenly remembered something I needed to do immediately in another room of the house, or, my normal default, lied.

I am probably not alone in flubbing the steps in my dance with honesty, sincerity, and self. My head knows this, but my heart still constructs battlements around itself to block soul mirrors wielded by my father or any-one else. I am most insincere with myself about what I need, what I want, what I desire, what I feel.

So many times, God, the lover of my soul, finds me in the labyrinth I have built around my heart and sits with me until I look up at Him. During a sermon, Lisa Harper of Elevation Church described a similar experience in her relationship with God, the summation of which is God saying to her, "I'm going to take you to the basement and sit with you in the dark until fear doesn't own you anymore." My response to hearing this is still, "Where did the floor go?"

I am reading *Desire* by John Eldredge as a devotional, after it sat in my Kindle queue for years; I never got past

"18%" complete every other time I started to read it. The book talks about how wrong it is to "kill" our desires, and how doing so is not the answer God intended on our oath to righteousness. I completely disagreed with this message when I was younger and couldn't get past my own blindness about who God really is. I couldn't process the truth of the message.

God is good like that: He knows when we can handle what we need. In my forties, I am finally learning how harsh and cruel I have been to my own heart. I was so focused on what I thought I should be doing with my life and the expectations of others that any time my heart whispered to me, I either shouted that whisper down with a "should," dissolved into a paralyzed puddle of guilt, or crushed my heart. I loved English but got a degree and a scholarship in engineering. I loved teaching but joined the military. I loved acting but only took a couple of classes and never pursued it as a hobby after I left college.

In the late '90s, I was so far down the road of convincing my heart it wanted nothing and needed nothing, I forgot what I liked. In another missing floor moment, I once told friends that I wouldn't go out to lunch with them because I didn't "like that restaurant" when, in truth, I didn't have the funds to eat out. I was struck speechless when they saw through my pretense and offered to pay for my meal. In this way, God has been faithfully and relentlessly riding wrecking balls through my labyrinth my whole life. He patiently and gently (for a wrecking ball) sits with me until I look up at Him, then He leads me to green pastures by still waters and restores my soul.

I learned later in my military career the sad truth about the phrase, "It's lonely at the top." I once worked on a special assignment with several subordinates, during which we had access to a communication system that allowed us to create chat rooms on our workstations. I found out all my subordinates were conversing in a chat room and joined it so I would be in on the jokes. Unfortunately, I made the mistake of commenting on something in the chat. Within fifteen minutes, I was the only one left in that room and my subordinates created another chat room which they never told me about and that I never found. I do not look too closely at how I feel about this memory, but it highlighted to me that I was walling myself off from something I truly wanted – community and companionship. I spent so many years convincing myself that I desired nothing and no one, that I was unable to fully face the resulting loneliness that came from crushing my heart.

Near the end of my Air Force career, I was deputy of a large unit returning from a six-month deployment. Buses brought us from the plane to where everyone else's family waited with open arms. Single and child-less, I dragged my six months' worth of luggage and gear towards my office, as close to death as I have ever been. Then I looked up and locked eyes with my brother (also military), who took time off from work and traveled to another city to welcome me home. In that moment, God once again saved my life.

God showed me once again that I am not alone, no matter how close to "the top" I get, that ignoring my desires does not give me power over them, that He sees and protects my true heart from the isolation I self-impose, and that He always has a ram (or a younger brother) on stand-by.

. . . .

Father God,

Open our eyes, our hearts, our minds, and our souls to Your amazing love. Shatter the lies that imprison us. Shatter the lies that con us into believing we are safe from hurt in isolation or that by avoiding relationships we can avoid pain. Let Your truth fill our minds, our hearts, and our hands and truly make us free to live fully and abundantly in fellowship that magnifies and brings glory to Your name. In Jesus' name, Amen!

. . . .

Jennine Carter is a degreed Civil Engineer, a 24-year veteran of the United States Air Force and an Online Women's eGroup Leader with Elevation Church. She resides in San Antonio, Texas, with a veritable forest of succulent plants, an eclectic collection of Anime DVDs, a craft room of phenomenal potential, a head shake-inducing quantity of office supplies, and entirely too much furniture for a single person. She believes the "Best is yet to come."

GOD MAKES
A HOME
for the lonely

He leads prisoners
into prosperity,

**only the rebellious
dwell in a parched land.**

Psalm 68:6

13

I MET GOD AT DISNEY
Sue Fattibene

God seems to enjoy communicating with me through signs, numbers, movies, music, and peacocks. When He sends them one after another, the message is especially powerful.

Two years after I moved from a traditional career into entrepreneurship as a life coach, we moved to Pittsburgh, where I knew no one. I worked from home helping people from the southeast U.S. and internationally, but not from the local area.

After fourteen months, I began asking God where to place my business office. I heard the date "January 5" and felt strongly that it meant the upcoming year. I prayed often about January 5 and as the date approached, I signed a contract to rent office space in a wellness center, specifically starting on January 5. I knew I was supposed to be in that center.

For two months, I paid rent, showed up, and had no new clients join me. I knew through the act of obedience there would be blessings, so I continued to be obedient with my office in this center, knowing that those who needed to be there would come.

In March, my husband and I took a trip to Disney World so he could attend a conference and I could attend a flower festival. I had waited years to attend this event and was so disappointed when rain was forecast for that entire day. I changed plans and made a reservation for High Tea at the Grand Floridian Resort & Spa, shifting from park mode to tea mode.

The resort was beautiful, and the ambiance was energetic with great shops and restaurants. A grand piano sat in the middle of the lobby and a brass band played on and off throughout the day in a balcony above the tearoom. High Tea was amazing, with scones, finger sandwiches, and desserts.

When I finished, I realized I still had some time left so I headed for a table and chair in the lobby to sit and think before heading back to the hotel. As I sat, I felt a wave of emotions. I was bothered by the work issues back home and had a silent conversation with God in the middle of the Grand Resort.

"God, I'm done!" I said.

"I'm exhausted trying to figure out how to start this business. I can't do it anymore."

I'm not sure what I thought I was quitting, but the issues with my business were really bothering me and I was considering closing my office doors.

God heard me because He stopped the rain outside, and the sun came out. I became QUITE agitated at seeing the sun when it was supposed to be raining. I started tearing up with all those thoughts in my head.

Then the pianist played a Disney song that I knew God meant for me: "When You Wish Upon a Star." He trailed off into another song that I recognized after a moment, the words tripping off my tongue— "Jesus, Jesus, Jesus, there's just something about that name. Master, Savior, Jesus, like the fragrance after the rain. Jesus, Jesus, Jesus, let all heavens and earth proclaim. Kings and kingdoms will all pass away, but there's something about that name."

The pianist finished that song and trailed back into the first. Then I was crying; I couldn't believe my eyes were officially leaking in this grand lobby. I realized God wanted me to know He heard me. Although I was not at the flower festival as planned, He gave me space to sit and talk with Him about the things that were bothering me. He listened and gave me the name Jesus to help me breathe. For Jesus was my "fragrance after the rain." The rain that had stopped me from attending the festival. He had reached down from the heavens to say, "I heard you Baby Girl! I've got this after the rain, and it is beautifully fragrant."

I caught up with my husband and his cohorts for dinner that night and when we walked into the dining area I almost passed out. The mirror behind the bar was adorned with an etched peacock from one side to the other. It was gorgeous. Large peacock feathers were woven into the carpet all along the floor.

The peacock is especially significant for me; whenever it has shown up, it represents the ultimate nod or attention-grabber from God. Every time a peacock has appeared, in whatever form, God has had a direct point or purpose for me. This one had massive grandeur.

I said, "WHOA! God, you are really trying to tell me something. What is it?"

I was brought to tears and my trust in our Father became very strong.

My answer came the next day. I left for the airport in the morning and received a text from the owner of the wellness center. She said I had a new client who wandered into the center, asked about coaching services, signed up, and would start the following week. I cried in laughter all the way to the airport. The client was my first of many at this new location and one I've grown especially close to.

I met God at Disney through wonders, music, and a peacock. I will NEVER forget my time with Him and the "fragrance after the rain" on that day. God knows the plans He has for us and will uphold us as we walk in blind faith and fragrant rain to reach the starting line of His purpose and plan for our lives.

I ask, Father, that only Your Holy Spirit will speak to me now as I wait on You for wisdom, insight, and direction. And whatever you show me or direct me to do, I pray that I will quickly obey. In Jesus's mighty name, Amen.

Sue E. Fattibene is a Certified "Reset" Life Coach, Business Strategist, Inspirational Speaker, Conference Creator, and Published Author with her book, "The Day the Angel Sat Beside Me." Her coaching program, "Reset! + Reboot! + Rev Up! ~ the Simple Unstuck Method," guides individuals on how to move from vision to accomplished with dreams, visions, goals, and callings both personally and professionally to successfully Rev Up! & Thrive in God's Design for Our Lives.

GIVE ME *your heart* and let your eyes DELIGHT **in my ways**

Proverbs 23:26

14

BUT FOR HIS GRACE AND MERCY

Breyuna Williams

We all have moments in life where we look back and think, if it wasn't for God, I don't know how I would have made it through. I've had several "But God" moments. Times when I know I only made it through because of God's grace and mercy.

As a strong-willed, independent woman, my "But God" moments are more than I'd like to admit. When asked to reflect on how God has directed my path throughout my life, a few stories really stick out. (Let's agree that there will be no judgment.)

As a teenager, I believed I was above reproach and, to be honest, many of my decisions were motivated by how much I could get away with and how deep the brow lines on my parents' foreheads would furrow.

My parents were strict. Raised in a Christian household, there were certain things that would not fly. Curfews for going out, curfews for talking on the phone, no boyfriends...rules, rules, and more rules. Things had to be done with decency and in order to stay under their roof. At fifteen, I'd had enough!

Thinking my life would be better if I went and lived somewhere else, I remember telling Big Mike to come and get me. Big Mike was smooth. His looks were not easy on the eyes, but all the girls liked him and, most importantly, trusted him. He was all too eager to "rescue" me from my parents' tight reign. As he headed to my house, some sense came to me, and I told him I couldn't go. Looking back on it, I realized that the "sense" I felt was God protecting me...guiding me to safe waters. With all of the current news about sex trafficking and kidnapping, so many things about that incident led me to believe that it was only because of God's grace and mercy that my life didn't go in a different direction.

My next "But God" moment happened after I had my oldest son. Postpartum depression syndrome is real. At the time, I didn't recognize what was going on nor did I want to accept that my future would consist of me being a single mother. My son's father and I had our issues. We were both immature and had things we needed to work on, but I believed that love would conquer all. I believed that love required doing what-ever you had to do in order to make it work, even if that meant being unhappy and sad. As long as I wasn't alone, I was ok.

One day my emotions got the best of me. As he drove up to drop off our son, I noticed there was another woman in the car. I immediately lost it. My anger was out of control.

At the end of it all, I found myself in the back of a police car heading to the police station...my legal career on the line. As I stood in front of the judge to plead my case, I remember hearing a voice from God say, "Be still, know that I the Lord God will fight your battles."

Although I had dug a really deep hole for myself, God's grace and mercy covered me. I stayed out of jail, my record expunged and I kept my bar license, providing me the opportunity to practice law for the last seven-teen years.

But God...

But God...

But God!

While reading this, I'm sure you can relate to these moments. Times when you know like you know that if it had not been for God on your side, your life would look quite different. As you look back, I encourage you to share your own "But God" moments.

Even in my current challenge of fighting Advanced Stage IV Breast Cancer, I know that this is just another "But God" moment. While I don't think God wants us to act foolish, be reckless, or feel like we have to face difficult times alone, He uses these moments to show us that He has our back and that only by His grace and mercy are we standing where we are today.

. . . .

Heavenly Father,

Thank You for Your grace and mercy. Thank You for Your love and for always watching over me. I know that if it had not been for Your grace and mercy, I would not be here today. Thank You Lord!

. . . .

Breyuna L. Williams is an Attorney and Producer. She has more than 10 years of legal and business experience helping filmmakers protect their intellectual property and produce high-quality, in-demand projects. As the managing member of the Law Offices of Breyuna L. Williams and President of Brewill Productions, she provides a wide array of services, including counseling clients on all aspects of non-patent intellectual property, trademark and copyright registration, prosecution, maintenance and enforcement, and financing creative innovation. Breyuna has served as production counsel for more than 50 projects advising clients from development through distribution.

But

GOD STILL LOVED US
with such

GREAT LOVE.

**He is so rich in
compassion and mercy.**
Even when we were dead
and doomed in our many sins,

HE UNITED US

**into the
very life of Christ
and saved us by**

his wonderful grace!

Ephesians 2:4-5

15

FORGIVENESS AND GRACE

Katherine James

We know what we know when we know it.

How can we expect someone to be who they haven't learned to be, to do what they haven't learned to do, and to say what they don't know how to say?

The absence of knowledge can cost us a lot and then, there is GRACE packaged in self-love.

I was a brand-new mom...Who am I kidding? That's the watered-down description. I was a SUPER mom, consumed with my precious little boy. I doted on and dressed him, played with, talked to, and loved on him.

I rarely put him down. Where I went, he went. If he couldn't go, I didn't want to go. If he wasn't welcomed, oh well. How I loved on my unparalleled gift from God.

One day, I noticed that my first love, my husband, and I were rarely together. Two ships passing in the night. He was seldom home, and I was always with "my" baby, my new love.

My new love and I were on another one of our many walks. The sun felt wonderful, everything was in bloom, oh the fresh air, and...I was frustrated, disappointed, and angry at the absence of my first love. My heart sank at the thought of the ever-growing distance between us. Why couldn't I remember the last time we walked as a family, played as a family? Had we ever walked as a family? Of course we did...didn't we?

My heart was heavy. Oh, how I wanted it to be the three of us again.

Shake it off girl, you got to do what you got to do. Junior is what matters most because he (my husband, my first love) is a full-grown adult who can take care of himself.

My insides were terrified, but I didn't know what to do about my first love. So, I gave Junior my all.

Oh, I remember, in the early days, we were a team of three. Quickly though, as I unknowingly pushed my first love out, we became two teams. We were kind enough to one another, we took care of the household business and lovemaking as needed, but we were no longer one. My first love became more distant and silent – his energies eventually redirected outward to his career and all that accompanied it. My energies lasered in a direction I could control (my new love). I didn't know what to do. I didn't know that there was something to do, because I didn't know what I had done.

We were high school sweethearts – fifteen and seventeen when we began dating. Friends who loved each other's company. Each of us came from large families with lots of examples of parents raising children. Yet, as first-time parents (twenty-five and twenty-seven years old) we were sinking within our sacred (secret) space, our little apartment. No one told us!

We loved each other but didn't know how to be with each other anymore. Other things and people had taken (or been given) our priorities. This reality led to tumultuous times in our marriage. We lived separate lives and didn't know how to get back to each other. We were heartbroken and didn't understand why this happened, when this happened, or even how it happened. We just knew that we were sad and lonely often. Love is NOT enough.

Although love wasn't a cure-all, it was the main ingredient that helped us to keep trying. We prayed, went to counseling, talked with pastors, loved ones, friends, cried, screamed (I screamed), worked with different techniques, diverted our energies with distractions, etc. We eventually – it took many years – found our bridge back to each other.

I had to give myself the gifts of forgiveness and grace over and over for introducing distance into our marriage. I had all but lost the love of my life and my actions placed us on that path. This was and is my truth. I didn't know what I didn't know, and that lack of knowledge almost cost me my first love.

Beloved, when you make a mistake, as we all do, give yourself grace and love. Do what you can to fix it, focus on what you can do now. Most importantly, be kind to yourself while you learn what to do. Love you well!

. . . .

Thank You Lord for loving me!

Help me to see and love myself the way You do. I release any guilt, shame, or condemnation I've held against myself. And, as I love myself, I love those around me. In Jesus' name, Amen.

. . . .

Dr. Katherine E. James celebrates thirty-eight years of marriage, her son, and her daughter in love. She loves God and functions as an associate pastor at Shiloh Deliverance Church International in Detroit, Michigan. Katherine serves as a licensed professional counselor, university and seminary professor, published author, speaker, community leader, and self-love transformational and freedom conductor. Katherine most treasures her relationships; therefore, she intentionally loves herself first to assure there is an overflow of love to share with others.

Love
THE LORD

with all
YOUR HEART

and with all
YOUR SOUL

and with all
YOUR STRENGTH

and with all
YOUR MIND;

Love your neighbor as yourself.

Luke 10:27

16

THE END OF ONE LIFE, THE BEGINNING OF A NEW ONE

Kenya Williams

I stopped by my mother's house with my baby girl one afternoon. I mentioned to my mother how tired I was and that I wasn't feeling well.

"Son, you need to get some rest – I'll watch the baby," she said.

Grateful, I left the baby with her, waved goodbye, and drove away.

As I was driving down the street, I had a fierce coughing spell. I coughed so hard it felt as if something exploded in my head. I felt a sharp, stabbing pain in my skull and then everything went black.

I woke up with my SUV on its side and struggled to get out, finally climbing out of the busted front windshield. With both adrenaline and blood flowing, I sat down on the side of the road. I was wondering what happened when a stranger wearing dark shades walked up to me.

"Are you ok? Can you move your arms?" he asked.

"Yes, sir," I replied.

"Wow! God surely is with you," he said, looking at my crumpled vehicle. "I'm going to call for help."

The accident happened on the side of a major thoroughfare in my town. Many people drove by and saw me sitting on the side of the road; some of those people happened to be cousins and other family members.

When the stranger saw my family had shown up, he said, "You really are in God's hands." He left, and I never saw or heard from him again.

When the ambulance arrived to transport me to the hospital, the responders told me I was lucky to be alive.

"Not too many people can walk away from a crash like

that," they said.

I was in shock and didn't have a clue what I had just survived. At the hospital, I watched as the doctor pulled glass, grass, and dirt out of my left arm. The nurse told me to count my blessings because I was blessed to be alive.

I was patched up with twenty-eight stitches on my left arm and five on my right hand, and the doctor told me I would have head trauma for the rest of my life.

He explained that my vehicle hit a tree, flipped three times, and landed on its side with. I still couldn't fully believe the severity of the crash until my mother and brother described the accident scene and showed me pictures of how badly damaged my car was.

I knew then that God has all power in His hands. That event changed how I look at life and its meaning.

I was down, alone, couldn't sleep, had no car, and no friends to call on. Reality can give you a different perspective. Analyzing everything that transpired, I gained a better understanding of what it means to live. I was thankful to be breathing and to see another day.

The Lord brought me through a horrific accident, and I know what it is to be born again. A part of me died in that crash and a part of me was reborn. No more was I feeling down, alone, and with no friends. I was blessed with the strength to carry on with a revived spirit.

After battling with the headaches, emotional pain, and suffering, I realized faith was the key to a long, prosperous life, so I understood why it all happened.

Everyone has their own purpose in life, and I have found mine because I could have died but the Lord kept me. I could have lost my arm, or my baby could have been in the vehicle that day. I carry a reminder on my arm every day – a scar that symbolizes a blessing to me, a reminder of how God spared my soul.

I am a believer in the Spirit because I know what hardship is like, feeling hopeless, wondering if things are going to get better. One thing is for certain: God is real. He will protect and cover you from all types of dangerous things in life.

I've come to the realization that trying to live and to do right leads to a rewarding life. My journey is proof because I'm a witness to how merciful God is. Life is not perfect but understanding that can be effective. This experience caused me to change for the better, for me and for my family. I cherish the little things in life, like waking up in the mornings, conversing with loved ones, taking a walk outside, and having dinner with family.

Surviving something like that will strengthen your relationship with God and family. I'm forever grateful for that experience because I know my life's importance. On that day, my life changed for the better because I'm stronger in spirit, mind, and soul. Even though the challenges in life are hard, I continue to trust and keep the faith. I've seen some things and I've lived them, too. Thank God I'm alive to share it with someone in need of inspiration. I hope my story can be an example of how to live.

....

Dear God,

Thank You for Your presence in my life. I know that in every situation—good or bad—You are with me. You are working things out for my good because I belong to You. I give You all praise, glory, and honor.
In Jesus' name, Amen.

....

Kenya Williams is an author who loves music, poetry, and films. As a little child, Kenya began to write stories and poems. Infatuated by music lyrics and creative writing, Kenya was inspired to become a lyricist and writer. The best source of expression for Kenya is spoken word, a craft he has developed through childhood, hoping to inspire people.

**And we know
that in all things**
GOD WORKS
FOR THE GOOD
OF THOSE
who love him,
**who have been
called according
to his purpose.**

Romans 8:28

17

TIME TO RELEASE

Ardra Tolbert Caldwell

One evening in 2016 while I was preparing for bed, I began to pray and ask God, "Am I on the path that You would have me to be?"

The thoughts that came to mind were not good, but I continued to pray, and the tears began to fall.

I had gone into a state of depression after my divorce six years earlier. Sleepless nights and unhappy thoughts plagued my life. Only my close circle of friends knew what I was dealing with internally. I was forty-two at the time and had been married for half of those years. I was the mother of a ten-year-old daughter and had no home to call my own. I was trying to wrap my brain around the idea of going from two homes that my ex-husband and I owned to living with friends after the divorce. My goal was to keep my daughter around familiar surroundings and keep her mentally well. For six years, I drifted, going through the motions of life to provide stability for my daughter while I kept my pain hidden.

On that morning in September 2016, I went to work as usual and checked my work email after settling in. I noticed an email from our HR department in response to a position I had applied for. Both excited and nervous, I opened it to find yet another letter saying, "Thank you for applying, but we have chosen another applicant to fill the position."

I felt discouraged and lost. I felt that my present employer was not allowing me to put my skills to work; my salary had been at a standstill for more than five years.

I was now a divorced mother of a teenager and barely making it in life. My day seemed to go downhill from there, and all types of emotions began to surface. I realized how much hurt and pain I had bottled up inside since my divorce, and I knew it was time for a change.

During my prayer that evening, I asked God to release all things that were holding me back from growth in all areas of my life. As I prayed, I began to feel a weight being lifted and my heart was overjoyed.

The release set me free!

Since 2016, my life has completely changed. I moved on to better employment with an incredible salary, earned my master's degree, and started two new businesses. My daughter will graduate from college in May 2022 and has started her own business. Unexpected blessings continue to shower down on my life.

Recently, God led me to birth my brand, "Celebrate The Release." Why? Once I let go of the disappointments, hurt, pain, and self-sabotage, the negativity was lifted, and I began to love myself again and help others. I am now experiencing joy and peace greater than I ever imagined possible.

Releasing is the start to entering a more flourished life, which will bring you complete understanding, joy, and peace within yourself. Fully releasing will provide you with the greatest self-satisfaction.

Is what you're holding on to keeping you from experiencing God's best in your life? Release it to God and let Him set you free.

Ardra Tolbert Caldwell is CEO/Founder of Celebrate The Release. Ardra is a graduate (1990) of Tuskegee University, BS in Social Work and a 2021 graduate of Columbia Southern University, Master of Public Administration. Ardra is the mother of Ardrianna Caldwell and Executive Assistant to the City Clerk of the City of South Fulton. Ardra is a people enthusiast who loves empowering people to grow, most importantly within themselves and then it can lead to empowering others.

So
if the
Son sets
you free,
YOU
will be free
indeed.

John 8:36

18

HIS WAY IS PERFECT

Tracy Mitchell

As the Fitness Center Manager at my church, I had to open at 5:30 a.m. each day—which meant I would wake up at 4 a.m. so I could get there in time to set up and run the center plus teach bootcamp each morning.

One morning, I was over it. My husband and eight-year-old daughter were sound asleep as I was leaving for work. I thought to myself, "This is crazy! Who does this? Is it even worth it?"

When I reluctantly arrived at work, a lady was waiting for me at the front door.

"I am so glad you showed up!" she said.

Woah.

Tears filled my eyes as I shared with her how I felt like quitting.

"Oh no!" she replied. "We need you!"

Her words stirred me up so much that I had the best day ever. I taught the bootcamp with more passion than usual, my joy was full, and I was refueled to continue my assignment for as long as God had me there.

This experience was a gentle reminder that I am called to serve others. Although there had been several times I wanted to cave in and quit, I was really going to do it this time.

It was just like God to keep me from falling and to send His word through one of His children. It was such a profound encounter, I use it as a reminder that no matter what things feel like, don't let your emotions rule and reign over you. It taught me to endure hardness and to trust that as for God, His way is perfect.

Since then, several people have shared testimonies about how I was used to make major differences in their lives. One member said I encouraged her to start her own business after I noticed she was passionate about picking berries and making jam and preserves for everyone for free. I ministered to her and said, "You could easily turn your passion into profit." She now is the owner of Joanne's Jars and sells her product in a few stores in Atlanta.

Another member told me I helped him to trust God again after doctors said they didn't know what type of disease he had and couldn't cure him. Someone else shared with me that I came into her life right on time and showed her that life is still worth living after the death of her grandson.

I am forever grateful that we serve a living God who is a very present help in our time of need, and when I really needed a boost of inspiration, He showed Himself strong on my behalf and provided exactly what I needed to run my race. Quitting is not an option for God's people. He makes the difference and the journey worthwhile.

....

Dear God,

I pray that the light of Christ in my heart may shine brightly. May I live in such a way that others may see the good works that I do in Your power and strength, and glorify You. In Jesus' name I pray, Amen.

....

Fitness Instructor Tracy Mitchell was born September 2, 1968, to entrepreneurs Robert and Loraine Johnson. The oldest of seven girls, Tracy is a natural born leader. She leads others to good health by inspiring them to put God's word in the workout. Widely known, her entrepreneurial spirit draws others. She has hosted fitness television shows, managed/directed fitness centers and health ministries. When Tracy is not empowering others, she spends time with her family, traveling and exploring new places.

LET
YOUR LIGHT
SHINE
BEFORE OTHERS

that they may see

your
good
deeds

AND GLORIFY
YOUR FATHER
IN HEAVEN.

Matthew 5:16

19

HE KNOWS THE PLAN

Lisa Antley

It's never too late to change your career path, but you need to wait on God. His timing is impeccable and makes all the difference.

I spent two and a half years working as a caregiver for one client, developing a close-knit relationship with him and his family. Although the job was good, the pay and benefits were not.

I began to grow restless and felt I could be doing something more -- helping more people. I went on a mad job hunt to find the "perfect" job, not really knowing what

I wanted to do or how I wanted to go about it. And although I received invitations for a few interviews, I didn't get hired.

Frustrated, I let go and gave up on the search for a while. I felt guilty because I knew my client and his family needed me, but I also wanted more for myself and my family.

I went to God in prayer with this dilemma and asked Him to lead and guide my job search -- to release me to a new job without any regrets. My patience and faith were tested because a year went by before He did just that. But when a new job did come to me, it happened easily because everything was in alignment with God's plan rather than my own.

I had started searching again and saw that a nearby nursing home facility was giving a free CNA class. Stepping out on faith, I put in my two-week notice and went for it.

Within a month, I passed the class, had an interview, and got the job. Of course, going from one client in a home health care setting to several residents in a nursing home took some getting used to, but three months later I'm still here, working and helping many. I also keep in contact with my former client and family, who have someone new and are doing well.

This experience made me grow closer in my relationship with God. He's always been there for me, even when I began to question whether He was during that long job search. I wanted the blessing quickly, but He gave it to me slowly and carefully when He knew I'd be ready for it.

I never would have thought I'd be working in a nursing home, especially during a pandemic. Nobody wants to get sick and although I had that fear, I am doing God's work and He protects me so I can continue doing it. I realize how blessed I am. I have my life, health, and strength. I will use it to comfort others in their time of need just as I would want someone to do for me.

Thank You, Lord,

for the good plans You have for me. Enlarge my vision of You and enable me to trust Your Word of truth through all the circumstances of my life, knowing that Your thoughts towards me are only good continually.

Lisa Antley is originally from Detroit, Michigan. She currently resides in Tennessee with her two daughters, Novia and Nadia. Lisa is a CNA dedicated to providing the best quality care for those in need. In her free time, Lisa enjoys family gatherings, listening to an eclectic selection of music, watching a variety of movies, taking snapshots with her camera, and being outside in the warmth of nature. Lisa's ultimate goal is to touch the lives of many through her written and spoken word.

"For I know the plans I have for you," declares the Lord, **"plans to**

PROSPER YOU

and

NOT TO HARM YOU

plans to give

YOU HOPE

and

A FUTURE.

Jeremiah 29:11

20

IN ALIGNMENT WITH YOUR ASSIGNMENT

Karen Skinner

I was tired and frustrated again, my head over a toilet, praying and crying. The fatigue was overwhelming. I constantly thought about how much I wanted to quit this job and do something enjoyable, something that would help further the Kingdom of God.

I was cleaning the toilet (a particularly smelly and dirty one) when I said to God, "I know you wanted me to start a business, Lord, but surely you have something far better for me than this!"

About six years prior, I was watching a Christian television program. As the evangelist preached, I felt God speaking to me about His plan for my life. The message created such excitement in me, and I knew straight away that I was meant to glorify God through business, even though I had very little business experience.

But bills were piling up, so I began working in a job that I didn't really want. I was grateful and enjoyed that position to a degree, but I had a strong yearning to own my own business. Eventually, this created in me an overpowering dissatisfaction that began to manifest itself in depression and weariness. It was so bad, I started to make bad mistakes. I began saying and doing things I wouldn't normally say or do, until one day, I was fired for the first time in my life.

The fact is, I believe God had wanted me to quit that job all along, but I was too afraid. I would say to God, "I am too old to find another job," or other similar excuses.

I felt ashamed and embarrassed, but at the same time I felt very relieved, and even happy to finally be free from that position!

The problem was that while I stayed employed there, God was unable to direct my path. I had been tying His hands by refusing to obey Him and quit. You know what they say: "You can't steer a parked car!" But through all of this, I knew God was working on my character.

I did eventually start a business – a cleaning business. I had wonderful clients who were all delighted with my services. BUT…even though I had a business, I was still unhappy because this wasn't what I was called to do. I had always wanted to do something creative and with purpose, and cleaning toilets just didn't satisfy that heartfelt longing.

In my spare time, I completed a Life Coaching certification and learned much about writing books, marketing, and creating digital products, courses, and websites. I couldn't believe how much I enjoyed it!

I had always hated anything to do with sales and marketing (or so I thought). But God knew what He had birthed inside of me.

I had discovered talents and gifts that I didn't know I had. I remembered the Scripture in Ephesians 2:10 NKJV, "For we are His workmanship, created in Christ Jesus for good works, which God prepared beforehand that we should walk in them."

I then realized that God had been preparing me all

along and that He has an assignment for everyone. I also knew I had to partner with God in my business, and not just run the business and hope that He would bless it. I knew He longed to work with me.

When I finally listened and obeyed the leading of the Holy Spirit, He was able to direct me to the specific assignment He had planned for me even before the foundation of the world. I now had a burning passion to help Christian female entrepreneurs discover their assignment and fulfill their passion and purpose for their lives.

As you begin to walk in your assignment, you will find that God supplies everything you need, whether it be finances, wisdom, resources, contacts, or divine appointments.

Ask God about your assignment. He has placed those passions and desires within you for a reason. I guarantee you won't regret it.

When you walk in your assignment, you are in God's perfect will for your life!

. . . .

**Lord, thank You for the assignment
You have for me.**

Help me to see and walk in Your purpose for my life.
Give me the courage to believe in what You have for me.
Amen.

. . . .

Karen Skinner is a certified Christian Life
Coach. Her passion is to help Christian
entrepreneur women build their online
brand and discover their God-given
assignment. Karen believes in partnering
with God in her business to help further
the kingdom of God while providing value
through branding and web-design products and services.

Many

are the plans
in a

PERSON'S
HEART,

but

it is the

LORD'S
PURPOSE
THAT PREVAILS.

Proverbs 19:21

21

LETTING GOD INTO YOUR CAREER

Patricia Ortega

Letting God into your career means surrendering it to His will, so you can enjoy the life you were created for.

God once told me I would be a counseling faculty at a community college. This was a big move from my staff position, but in faith, I resigned from the secure, well-paying job I loved. Days later, a friend called and offered me an amazing position making $80,000 to start. It was surreal, but it wasn't the counseling position the Lord had promised. It took every bit of me to turn down that job; I was making less than half the salary at the time and wondered whether I was being unreasonable. Had I heard God correctly?

Before my last day in my staff position, I went to an orientation for a part-time counseling role. I had the education, having earned an MS in counseling, but during the orientation I was told that no one was hired for full time faculty positions without two-plus years of adjunct faculty experience at a variety of campuses. That was ok; I wasn't concerned with the timeline because I was surrendered to God's will.

Still, I wasn't sure how I'd pay rent. Where was I going to live, God?

On my last day, I got a voicemail, "Hi Patty, I know that you love your job, but we have a need in our department and you're the person we're hoping for... might you be willing to work one, maybe two days a week?"

This God-sent caller was one of my dear mentors from an internship I had five years earlier at the campus of my dreams. He had no idea I submitted a resignation; we hadn't spoken in years. This part-time opportunity alone would replace my paycheck.

I was overwhelmed with emotion and gratitude. He

kept His word. God is real.

I took bold action and moved closer to this dream campus of mine to be in position for God's will – the full-time faculty role I knew was coming.

Six months later, a position did come up and I applied. For a woman who cried at her first interview, I found it interesting that God was so tangibly with me. I felt humbly confident relying on Him. Still, despite the sharp competition, the Lord fought my battle and gave me the offer.

Being surrendered involved letting go of an $80,000 position, not being swayed by the circumstances or the timeline, and moving in faith at all stages of the process. It meant giving up my will to submit to God's plan for my life.

Since becoming a faculty member, I have taught, counseled, and helped people of all ages and in all stages make successful education, life, and career moves. Today, I also love helping others surrender their career to God and bring their faith to work.

It's a wonderful feeling to know you are in His will. There is peace in all you do, God's favor is all around, and He makes all things work for the good of us who love Him.

The Lord is no respecter of persons, and He has a plan for you too. Imagine living life on the wings of eagles, taking leaps of faith, and working unto the Lord! I pray you consider what it would be like to co-labor with Christ and surrender your life – and career – to His will. I pray that you would let the love of Christ shine through into your heart, your mind, and your actions, so that the work you do can impact the people around you.

· · · · · · · ·

Dear Heavenly Father,

I humbly come before You, thanking You for every provision You've gifted me with. May I always acknowledge You as my source and my Lord, heeding The Holy Spirit's guidance for every decision I make. I thank You for Jesus Christ, that through His work on the cross, You welcome me as Your child, and that as Your child, I can trust You for my present and my future. Help me to walk this life trusting in Your love and provision for me. In Jesus' name, Amen.

· · · · · · · ·

Patricia Ortega is a speaker, coach, and founder of The Uncommon Career. Running into her own barriers to the work world, she made "career" her career, and for the last decade has helped others succeed in preparing for, launching, and changing professions. Patricia holds a Bachelor of Science in business administration, and Master of Science in counseling. She landed her own 6-figure position with The Lord's guidance, and with the mindset, strategies, and techniques she now teaches others.

in the Lord

with

ALL YOUR HEART

and

LEAN NOT ON YOUR
OWN UNDERSTANDING;

in all your ways

submit to Him,

and He will make

MAKE YOUR
PATHS
STRAIGHT.

Proverbs 3:5-6

22

MISSED SIGNALS
Lesa Dale

Sometimes we're so focused on our own ideas or distracted by life that we miss the signals God sends us. He tried to get my attention for several years, and I didn't hear it.

I've been doing business online for a long time, going back to 1999 when I worked in the main office of an online shopping MLM company. After I left there, I tried a little bit of everything: I taught myself how to hand-code HTML to create websites, ran a small printing company, did graphic design, and trained as a virtual assistant and a Christian life coach. I did all that while also raising three kids, two of whom I homeschooled.

I started a coaching program for teens to help them find ways to make money online. It was business coaching for teenagers, and a few years into that, I added the concept of using their spiritual gifts to help them find an entrepreneurial direction.

Then I got distracted. I married and let the business take a back seat, "playing" at doing business for a few years. I helped a couple of friends build websites, printed wedding invitations as gifts to several brides, and started leading our homeschool cover school and co-op group. I was very "busy," but I didn't have direction. I let life take me where it would.

When my oldest son, Dustin, decided to return to school to play football, I had him take a placement test and an aptitude assessment to ensure he was where he needed to be. I was stunned by the results that my big, athletic son would make a great accountant. Had they met him? It didn't match what I knew about my boy.

Later, when Dustin was graduating high school, our church walked everyone through the DISC personality profile and spiritual gifts assessments again. I had Dustin go through the process and discovered that his gifts and personality aligned with accounting. Who knew! But as I realized a few years later, this was not the whole picture.

With this third reoccurrence of spiritual gifts, I knew God was trying to get my attention. As my youngest son, Kenny, was entering high school, I began preparing myself to become an empty nester; I started working out the kinks of a new coaching business.

I started teaching a career prep class at our co-op, taking those kids through many personality assessments and using other tools to help them identify their gifts, personalities, and strengths. I started putting the pieces together and learned what had been missing in the assessments for my older son. That experience helped me develop "Discerning My Calling," which became my focus. The trend at the time was to use your name as the website, and I had snagged LesaDale.com a few years earlier, using that to create my business.

Late in 2018, as I prepared for the new year, I spent a lot of time listening, looking for goals, words, and verses to carry me through the following year. God gave me the word "discover," so I spent a lot of time in 2019 discovering how to partner with God in my business to become a Kingdom Entrepreneur.

As I was preparing for a workshop, God told me that he had been trying to get my attention for several years. He kept bringing up spiritual gifts with personalities and business. He told me to run my business and do my coaching the way He had prepared me to, not the way of the world.

Finally, I heard that it wasn't all about me. It was about Him, and we needed a new name; thus, I changed the name of my business from my name to Life Walk GPS.

As a Christian business and life coach, speaker, and author, I am doing what God created me to do. My gifts, personality, and strengths are all in alignment with His calling for my life. I bounced from job to job, business idea to business idea, until I started listening to God and allowed Him to give me the confidence and clarity of His direction.

Romans 11:29 says that the gifts and the calling of God are irrevocable. That word, irrevocable, defined -- not to be revoked or recalled; unable to be repealed or annulled; unalterable. The gifts and the calling of God are irrevocable. Our gifts and our calling are irrevocable.

I believe God created each of us with a unique combination of gifts, personalities, and strengths to fulfill the destiny He created us to accomplish according to His purpose. We are to thrive in our lives, business, and ministry while creating a legacy of abundance and good works for His glory.

. . . .

Father,

We know Your gifts and calling are irrevocable. Even though You have given us free will to make choices, You know what our choices will be, and You have made plans to bring those choices to work for Your good and purpose. Thank You, Father, for using my decisions for Your kingdom's purpose. Amen

. . . .

Lesa Dale is a contemporary Christian Business and Life Coach trained in Spiritual Gifts/DISC alignment. She is the founder of LifeWalkGPS™, where she engages Christians ready to transition from unsure to confident by allowing them to identify the purpose God has for them based on their unique gifts, personalities, and strengths to create the Kingdom life, business, or ministry God designed them to build.

**For the gifts
and the calling of God
are irrevocable**

for

HE DOES
NOT WITHDRAW

what He has given

nor

DOES HE
CHANGE HIS MIND

about those to whom

HE GIVES HIS GRACE

or

to whom

HE SENDS
HIS CALL

**Romans 11:29
(AMP)**

A SPECIAL INVITATION

Before we end, I want to share something with you...

Last year, I rode a one-eyed horse named China.

Those who know me know that animals terrify me. My fear of animals is so intense that being within even one hundred feet of them freaks me out.

So, what made me mount this (surprisingly gentle) two-ton beast?

Something more important than my fear...my sixteen-year-old nephew.

Ishmael loves animals and wanted to celebrate his birthday at a horse farm. When I first learned of his plans, I decided I would go and watch everyone else ride from an appropriate distance away. But, when we arrived at the farm, my nephew begged me to fully engage in the festivities by riding a horse.

He said, "Getting on a horse will be a gift to me."

To me, it sounded like, "Getting over your fear will be a gift to me." Somehow my desire to bring joy to my nephew became bigger than my fear.

I rode China around the pasture, arms shaking, legs trembling, and heart racing, with a big smile on my face. My fear didn't go away, it was just no longer a controlling factor.

I ended up really enjoying myself and the experience prompted so many stories to tell. I could fill an entire book telling you about the serendipity of a visually impaired girl riding a one-eyed horse.

But for now, I just wanted to leave you with this...

The fear doesn't have to go away before you act. For way too long, I've avoided potentially life-changing experiences because I thought I had to get over my fears first. Now, I'm embracing the idea that I can feel the fear and do it anyway!

Have you ever acted in spite of your fear? I'd love to be inspired by your stories!

Inspirational Devotionals is a collaborative book project where I am bringing together inspirational storytellers from all walks of life to share stories that uplift the spirit, enlighten the mind, and warm the heart.

Our upcoming books will feature stories of choosing faith over fear and triumph over seemingly insurmountable obstacles.

I'm looking for passionate, purpose-filled individuals who are called to transform lives with their stories and knowledge.

If that's you, apply to be a part of the next Inspirational Devotionals collaborative book project!

AN INVITATION TO FAITH-FUELED COACHES, CONSULTANTS, ENTREPRENEURS, AND MINISTRY LEADERS

Transform your story into a powerful inspirational message!

If you want to impact and inspire lives with your story, apply to be a co-author in the upcoming Inspirational Devotionals collaborative book project.

InspirationalDevotionals.com/apply

71043764R00086